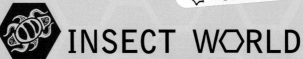

INSECT W⬡RLD

HORNETS

SANDRA MARKLE

INCREDIBLE INSECT ARCHITECTS

LERNER PUBLICATIONS MINNEAPOLIS

FOR CURIOUS KIDS EVERYWHERE

ACKNOWLEDGMENTS

The author would like to thank Dr. Kevin Foster, Harvard University, for sharing his expertise and enthusiasm. The author would also like to thank Dr. Simon Pollard, Curator of Invertebrate Zoology at Canterbury Museum, Christchurch, New Zealand, for his help with the scientific name pronunciation guides. Finally, a special thanks to Skip Jeffery, who shared the effort and joy of creating this book.

Lerner Publications Company
A division of Lerner Publishing Group, Inc.
241 First Avenue North
Minneapolis, MN 55401 USA

For reading levels and more information, look up this title at www.lernerbooks.com.

Library of Congress Cataloging-in-Publication Data

Markle, Sandra.
     Hornets : incredible insect architects / by Sandra Markle.
        p.   cm. — (Insect world)
     Includes bibliographical references and index.
     ISBN 978–0–8225–7297–8 (lib. bdg. : alk. paper) 1. Hornets—Juvenile
     ISBN 978–0–7613–4006–5 (EB pdf)
  literature. I. Title.
  QL568.V5M37 2008
  595.79'8—dc22   2007022290

Manufactured in the United States of America
9-42062-8132-4/29/2016

CONTENTS

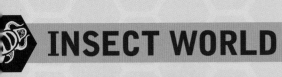
WELCOME TO THE WORLD OF INSECTS—

those animals nicknamed bugs. It truly is the insects' world. Scientists have identified more than a million kinds—more than any other kind of animal. And they're everywhere—even on the frozen continent of Antarctica.

So how can you tell if what you see is an insect rather than a relative, like the centipede *(right)*? Both belong to a group of animals called arthropods (AR-throh-podz). The animals in this group share some features. They have bodies divided into segments, jointed legs, and a stiff exoskeleton. This is a skeleton on the outside, like a suit of armor. But the one sure way to tell if an animal is an insect is to count its legs. All adult insects have six legs, and they're the only animals in the world with six legs.

This book is about a kind of winged insect called a hornet. A hornet works with its family to design and build an amazing home.

HORNET FACT

Like all insects, a hornet's body temperature rises and falls with the temperature around it. Hornets sometimes have to work to keep their house from getting too hot or too cold.

OUTSIDE AND INSIDE

ON THE OUTSIDE

Some people confuse hornets and wasps. It's easy to tell the difference, though. Compare the Asian giant hornet to the potter wasp. Both hornets and wasps have two big eyes. But a hornet's head is larger. Both have a skinny waist, but the hornet's waist is shorter.

Not all kinds of hornets are bigger than all kinds of wasps. But the Asian giant hornet is. It is the largest kind of hornet—about 2 inches (5 centimeters) long with a 3-inch (8 cm) wingspan.

Although some wasps are nicknamed hornets, the only true hornet in the United States is the European hornet. No one knows how it arrived from Europe, its natural home. It was first found in New York State in 1840. Since then it has spread throughout the eastern states and as far west as the Dakotas.

HORNET FACT

The Asian giant hornet's stinger is extra big too—about a quarter of an inch (0.6 cm) long. Like all hornets, though, these giants only sting to defend their nest or kill prey.

HORNET

WASP

Take a look at this female European hornet. Its body feels like tough plastic. Instead of having a hard, bony skeleton on the inside the way you do, an insect has an exoskeleton. This hard coat covers its whole body—even its eyes. The exoskeleton is made up of separate plates connected by stretchy tissue. That lets it bend and move. Check out the other key parts that all hornets share.

ABDOMEN

THORAX

HEAD

ANTENNA: This is one of a pair of movable feelers. The hornet uses these to sense size and shape while building the family's nest. Hairs on the antennae and on other body parts detect chemicals for taste and smell.

MANDIBLES: These are hard, toothlike jaws on the outside of the mouth. They are used to bite, scrape, and dig.

SIMPLE EYES: These small eyes sense only light and dark. They help the hornets

A hornet has a stinger that injects venom.

WINGS:
A hornet has two pairs of wings. Hind or back wings are connected to front wings by hooks. This lets the sets of wings beat together to power flight. Both pairs are attached to the thorax.

LEGS AND FEET:
These are used for walking and holding on. All legs are attached to the thorax. Long hind legs launch the hornet into the air for flight.

SPIRACLES:
These holes down the sides of the thorax and abdomen let air into and out of the body for breathing.

COMPOUND EYES:
What look like big eyes are really hundreds of eye units packed together. They can look in every direction at once.

Now look inside a hornet queen, the member of the family that produces young.

BRAIN: This receives messages from the antennae, eyes, and sensory hairs. It sends signals to control all body parts.

ESOPHAGUS: Food passes through this tube between the mouth and the crop. The esophagus is too narrow for anything but liquid food.

NERVE CORD: This is the insect's nervous system. It sends messages between the brain and other body parts.

Approved by Dr. Kevin Foster, Harvard University

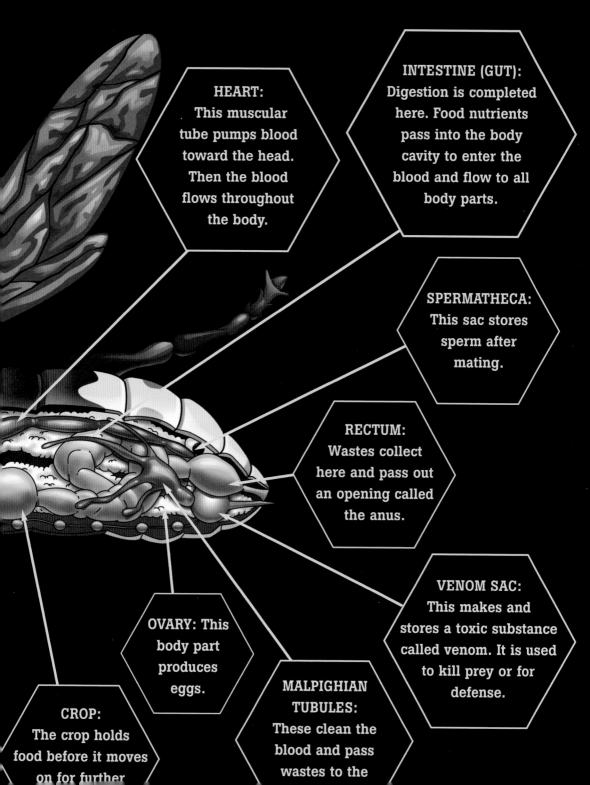

HEART:
This muscular tube pumps blood toward the head. Then the blood flows throughout the body.

INTESTINE (GUT):
Digestion is completed here. Food nutrients pass into the body cavity to enter the blood and flow to all body parts.

SPERMATHECA:
This sac stores sperm after mating.

RECTUM:
Wastes collect here and pass out an opening called the anus.

VENOM SAC:
This makes and stores a toxic substance called venom. It is used to kill prey or for defense.

OVARY: This body part produces eggs.

MALPIGHIAN TUBULES:
These clean the blood and pass wastes to the

CROP:
The crop holds food before it moves on for further

BECOMING AN ADULT

Insect babies grow into adults in two ways: complete metamorphosis (me-teh-MOR-feh-sus) and incomplete metamorphosis. Metamorphosis means change. Hornets develop through complete metamorphosis. Their life includes four stages: egg, larva, pupa, and adult. Each looks and behaves very differently. Here you can see three stages of a European hornet's life cycle.

IN INCOMPLETE METAMORPHOSIS, insects go through three stages: egg, nymph, and adult. Nymphs are much like small adults. But nymphs can't reproduce.

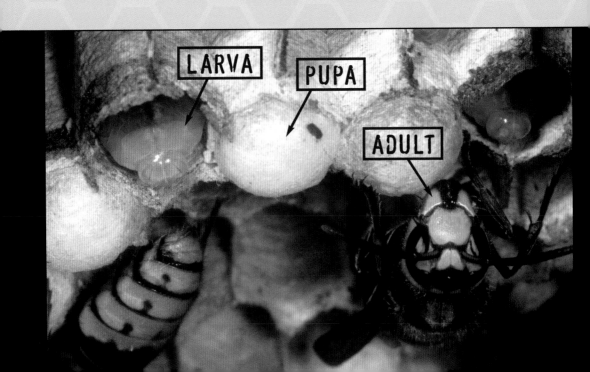

LARVA

PUPA

ADULT

The focus of adult hornets' lives is building the family's nest. It's something they just naturally know how to do. The results are truly amazing. The hornets shape their nest to fit into the space the queen chooses. They build it, one cell at a time, from flakes of paper they make themselves. Even though they take turns building, each cell is always a perfect six-sided shape—a hexagon. When there is no room on one level, the hornets add more floors to their nest. Each new floor hangs below the one above. The hornets also build and remodel the outside of the nest. They make sure the nest is always wrapped in layers of paper. This covering protects it from the weather.

A PERFECT NEST SITE

The nest is begun by just one hornet—the queen. She is the architect who starts the nest's design. She also chooses the building site. This is a place sheltered from wind and rain. It has to be close to food like ripening fruit or flowers. She'll need to eat the sweet liquid plants produce while she builds. The building site she chooses is also out of the reach of predators—like raccoons, skunks, and birds—that eat hornets.

When a hornet queen starts building depends on the weather. This queen lives in North America where winters are cold. She spent the winter hibernating or in a kind of sleep. As spring warms up, she crawls out of her resting spot in a rotted log.

After warming in the sunshine, she takes flight. She searches first for flowers. From these she gets a meal of sugary liquid nectar. Then she flies off. She flies past the empty nest where she grew up. Nests usually are used for only one year. The queen flies until she finds a hollow space in a house wall. This is the perfect place for her nest.

HORNET FACT

Hornets have been clocked flying at a speed of 19 feet (6 meters) per second.

A STRONG BUILDING MATERIAL

The hornet queen needs a strong, lightweight material to build the nest. She creates this herself. First, she looks for an old tree stump. She scrapes off a mouthful of wood fibers with her mandibles. She chews the fibers. This mixes them with her saliva, the juices in her mouth. She also stops to scoop up bits of sand.

Back inside the house wall, she presses this mouthful on the nest site's ceiling. The wood paste she makes dries and becomes hard. She repeats the process, shaping each bit of paste with her mandibles and feet. Mouthful by mouthful, she makes a short, strong pedicel (PED-eh-sel), or post, hanging from the ceiling.

The queen makes more trips to scrape up mouthfuls of wood. But she doesn't add sand. Each new mouthful makes a flake of paper. She shapes the paper flakes, one at a time. And she uses them to build the first cell of her nest.

HORNET FACT

The hornet's paper often looks striped. That's because the hornet collects wood fibers from different kinds of trees—each with its own unique color.

MANY SMALL ROOMS

The hornet queen builds the first level of the nest one paper cell at a time. Each cell is a perfect six-sided shape—a hexagon. A cell of this shape is roomy but doesn't take up much space. The hornet queen uses each of the sides of a cell as the wall of another cell. This way she doesn't have to use as much paper to build a group of cells. Soon the queen has a comb of 12 cells hanging—open ends down—from the pedicel. Best of all, the cells are just the right size for the young hornets that will grow inside them.

After she completes the nest's first cluster of cells, the hornet queen lays eggs. She sticks one inside each cell. It will take nearly a week for her eggs to hatch. While she waits, she flies out to feed on fruit juice and nectar. She never goes very far or stays away for very long. She needs to defend her eggs from predators, such as ants and spiders.

CARING FOR THE YOUNG

HUNGRY BABIES

When the larvae hatch, they are tiny. In fact, they are so tiny it seems they might slip out of the nest. But they give off a sticky liquid that glues them into their cells. And, day by day, the larvae eat and grow bigger.

Like adult hornets, the larvae have an exoskeleton. When a larva grows too big, its exoskeleton no longer fits. Then the exoskeleton splits open, and the larva molts, or sheds its covering. There is already a new protective coat underneath. It's soft at first, though. So the larva swallows air to stretch its new exoskeleton before it hardens. This gives it a little extra room to grow before it has to molt again. After just a few molts, the larvae are so big they fill their cells. Then there is no more danger of them falling out of the nest.

Big or small, the larvae are always hungry. They scratch the sides of their paper cells with their jaws, begging to be fed. *Gruuu! Gruuu! Gruuu!* The noise gets louder and louder as more of the larvae join in. Hearing them, the hornet queen flies off again and again. She keeps busy hunting for food for her hungry brood.

HORNET FACT

When larvae molt, they often eat their old skin. They need the food value it has. Larvae will molt about five times before they're ready to become adults.

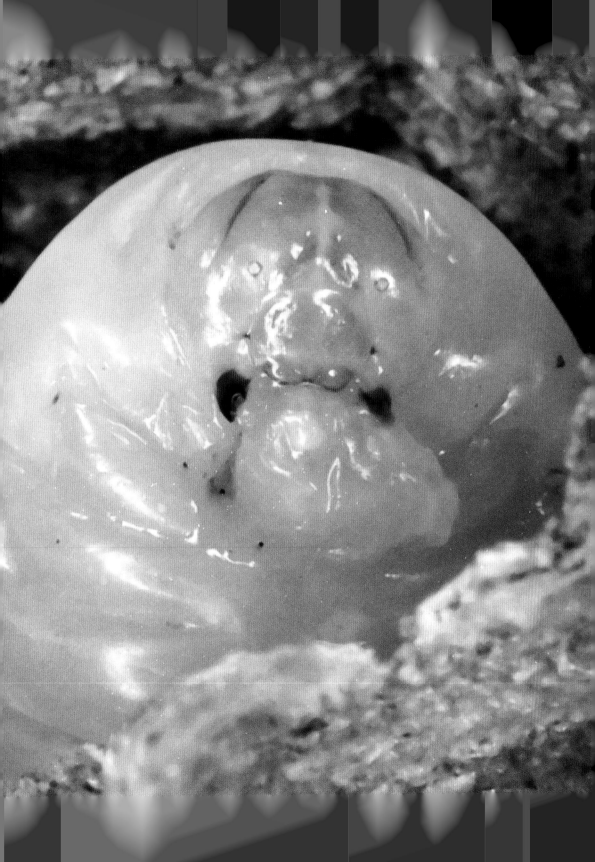

HUNTING FOR FOOD

The queen swoops down over a patch of flowers. With her compound eyes, she can look in all directions at once. She spots a honeybee and chases after it. When the honeybee lands, the hornet queen drops onto its back. She grabs the bee, moves it into position, and bites off its head. Next, she bites off the bee's abdomen. What's left is the bee's thorax. That's all she wants. The queen crushes the exoskeleton of the bee's thorax with her strong jaws. Then she pulls out the flight muscles. The flight muscles are a rich source of protein. The larvae need protein to grow and develop.

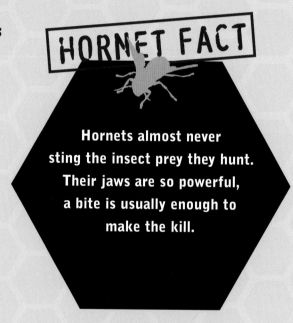

HORNET FACT

Hornets almost never sting the insect prey they hunt. Their jaws are so powerful, a bite is usually enough to make the kill.

EVERYONE EATS

As she flies home, the hornet queen chews up the meat. But she doesn't swallow any herself. Her esophagus is so narrow only droplets of liquid can pass through. Besides, she's unable to digest solid protein like this meat. When she arrives home, she tears the meatball apart and feeds it to the larvae. When the larvae were little, she took time to stop at nearby orchards or flowering plants for a meal of nectar. But the larvae are nearly full grown, so they can feed her. She touches first one and then another with her antennae. Each larva responds by bringing up a drop or two of a sugary, protein-rich liquid for her to eat. This way the hornet queen and her brood feed each other.

HORNET FACT

The hornet's food gives it energy to fly for long periods. Companies in Asia and Europe have created energy drinks that they claim have the same chemicals that are in the liquid made by hornet larvae.

CHANGES ARE COMING

The larvae eat and grow bigger for about two weeks. Then they are ready for the next stage of their life cycle. Each larva uses a special gland on its head to spin silk threads. It keeps spinning until it makes a silken cap that covers the opening of its paper cell. Safe inside its cell, the larva goes through its pupa stage.

As a pupa, it does not eat. And it does not make noise. But inside the cell, its body shape is changing. So is the way all of its body systems work. The pupa is turning into an adult hornet. The young adults on the next page have chewed open the silk caps on their cells. They are crawling out.

HORNET FACT

The young workers the hornet queen produces are all females.

BUILDING THE WORKFORCE

It's time for the hornet colony to get bigger. The new adults go to work. Now the queen's whole job is to lay eggs. And every egg has to have its own cell. The new adult workers add onto the nest. They keep on building until the nest stretches from wall to wall inside the sheltered space. Soon the nest is full of worker eggs, larvae, and pupae.

HORNET FACT

Each cell is reused about four times. Then it is left empty.

The queen stays home laying eggs. The workers continue to enlarge the nest. They also hunt and bring home prey to feed the larvae. This worker just caught a long-horned beetle.

BUILDING A WORKING NEST

KEEPING THE AIR CLEAN

The hornet workers build two more pedicels. Each hangs down from the first comb. The workers start building a second level of cells below the first. Instinct makes them separate the layers of the comb this way. But it's a good design feature. It allows air to flow freely around the cells. That clears the nest of carbon dioxide, the waste gas all animals breathe out. A nest with too much carbon dioxide could be poisonous for the hornets. The workers add more and more floors. They keep building until the nest looks like an upside-down wedding cake.

HORNET FACT

To keep the nest clean, workers remove waste droppings and dead hornets. They carry these out of the nest and drop them. A garbage dump piles up under the nest.

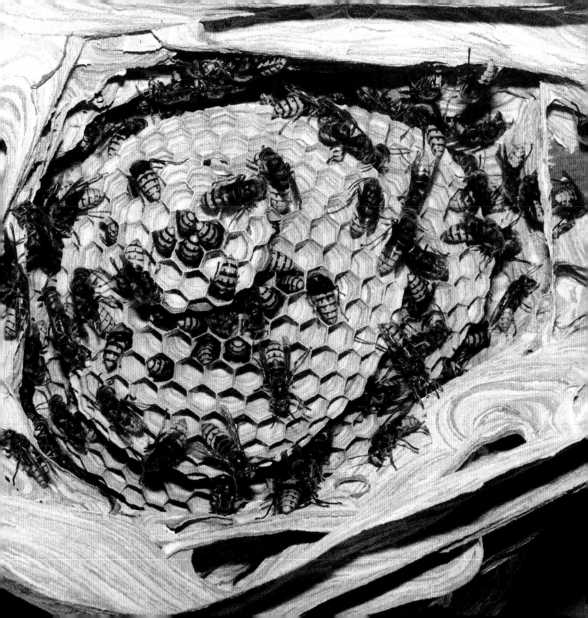

STAYING WARM

The workers also add onto the layers of paper that cover the nest. These protect the nest from rain and wind. They also help control the temperature inside the nest. The larvae develop best when the air temperature around them is about 83°F (28°C). The air outside may cool below that at night. Active hornets give off body heat, though. The paper layers around the nest trap this heat, so the nest stays warm.

HORNET FACT

At its peak size in late summer, a hornet's nest is likely to be home to 700 or more workers.

COOLING THE NEST

In summer, when the air heats up, the nest may get too hot. To cool it, workers fan their wings. This moves the air more quickly between the outside and inside of the nest. If the temperature still rises, the workers fly out to collect mouthfuls of water. They drop them on the nest's surface and fly off for more. Mouthful by mouthful, they will soak the surface of the nest. As the water evaporates, or changes into water vapor, it cools the nest. If you've ever felt cool after a swim or bath, you've learned how well the hornet's effort works.

HORNET FACT

When fanning, a group of hornets space themselves around the nest entrance and all face outward. Then they all beat their wings at the same speed. After about three minutes, another group takes over.

DEFENDING THE NEST

As the hornets build their nest, they make openings. These let air flow in and out. They also build a main entrance. Some workers are always on guard at the entrance. They will defend this opening from predators such as ants, spiders, or even other hornets.

Hornets have a strong sense of their home nest's smell. When any living thing comes to the nest opening, the workers on guard check its smell. If it doesn't smell familiar, they attack. The hornets defending the nest also release pheromones, special scents. Other hornet workers detect this alarm. They rush to join in the attack. The workers sting again and again to drive the enemy away or kill it.

HORNET FACT

Giant Asian hornets use their alarm pheromone to mark a beehive. Honeybees are prey for these hornets. And this scent guides their nest mates to the hive.

A NEW COLONY

In September, the queen lays special eggs. The larvae that hatch from them develop as usual. But they grow up to become young queens and male hornets. These adults fly away, pair off, and mate. The males die shortly after mating. The queens find places where they can hibernate. That way they escape the cold winter weather. The old queen, though, doesn't hibernate. When the weather turns cold, she dies.

With no queen, no new eggs are being laid in the nest. Workers live for only three to four weeks, so the hornet family soon becomes smaller. Finally, the nest the family worked so hard to build is empty. It will never be used again.

The hornet family isn't really finished, however. In the spring, the young queens will crawl out of their hiding places. They will fly off in search of building sites. When a young queen finds one, she'll start the nest that a whole new generation of hornets will build together.

HORNETS AND OTHER INSECT ARCHITECTS

HORNETS BELONG TO A GROUP, or order, of insects called Hymenoptera (hi-men-NOP-ter-ra). That name comes from the Greek words for membrane and wings. It refers to the hornet's transparent wings. This order includes hornets, wasps, ants, and bees. There are more than 100,000 different kinds of Hymenoptera. They are the third-largest group of insects after Coleoptera (KOH-lee-ap-tuh-ruh)—which includes beetles, weevils, and fireflies—and Lepidoptera (lep-eh-DOP-ter-ruh)—the order of butterflies and moths.

SCIENTISTS GROUP living and extinct animals with others that share the same features. In this system of classification, hornets belong to the following groups:

> kingdom: Animalia
> phylum: Arthropoda (ar-throh-POH-da)
> class: Insecta
> order: Hymenoptera

HELPFUL OR HARMFUL? Hornets are both. Hornets kill harmful insects such as ticks and houseflies that spread diseases. Hornets also carry pollen from flower to flower so plants can reproduce. However, hornets are harmful because they kill honeybees. Honeybees pollinate farmers' crops and produce honey. Hornets also bite and damage some fruit to get the sweet juice. Many people are afraid of hornets because their sting is painful.

HORNET QUEEN
ACTUAL SIZE

MORE INSECT ARCHITECTS

Other insects also build homes. Compare these insects to hornets. Check out their nest-building skills.

Tailor ants work together to build a shelter. Some of the ants hold the edges of a leaf together. Then other ants hold their larvae against the leaf and squeeze them. The larvae give off sticky silk strands that stitch the leaf edges together. This makes a simple shelter where the queen lays her eggs. More leaves are added to the shelter as the ants' nest grows bigger.

Female **potter wasps** work alone to build a nest of mud and water. This nest may have just one cell or several. After the nest is built, the female goes hunting for insect larvae or spiders. She captures one for each cell she built. Paralyzing her prey with a sting, she carries it home. She pushes this prey into a cell and lays an egg in the cell. Then she seals the opening. When the larva hatches, the prey becomes its food supply. After it goes through the pupa stage, the young adult breaks out of its cell.

Honeybees work as a family to build a hive, a home made of connected six-sided cells. Like hornets, honeybees make their own building material, but the bees make wax not paper. As with hornets, a queen lays eggs for the hive's cells. The developing larvae are tended by workers. Workers also continue to add more cells to the hive.

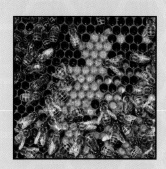

GLOSSARY

abdomen: the tail end of an insect. It contains systems for digestion and reproduction.

adult: the final stage of an insect's life cycle

antennae: movable, jointed parts on the insect's head used for sensing

brain: receives messages from the antennae, eyes, and sensory hairs. It sends signals to control all body parts.

complete metamorphosis: a process of development in which the young look and behave very differently from the adults. Stages include egg, larva, pupa, and adult.

compound eyes: big eyes are really hundreds of eye units packed together. These let it look in every direction at once.

crop: area of the digestive system where food is held before it is passed on for further digestion

egg: a female reproductive cell; also the first stage of an insect's development

esophagus (ee-SAH-feh-gus)**:** a tube through which food passes from mouth to crop or stomach

exoskeleton: protective, skeleton-like covering on the outside of the body

head: the insect's body part that contains the mouth, the brain, and sensory organs, including the eyes and the antennae, if there are any

heart: muscular tube that pumps blood

hibernate: a sleeplike state that lets the insect escape harsh weather conditions

incomplete metamorphosis: a process of development in which the young look and behave much like a small adult, except that they are unable to reproduce. Stages of life include egg, nymph, and adult.

intestine (gut): digestion is completed here. Food nutrients pass into the body cavity to enter the blood and flow to all body parts.

larva: the stage between egg and pupa in complete metamorphosis

Malpighian (mal-PEE-gee-an) **tubules:** the organ that cleans blood and passes wastes to the intestines

mandibles: the grinding mouthparts of an insect

molt: the process of an insect shedding its exoskeleton

nerve cord: the nervous system. It sends messages between the brain and other body parts.

ovary: the body part that produces eggs

pheromones: chemical scents given off as a form of communication

predator: an insect that is a hunter

prey: an insect that a predator catches to eat

pupa: at this stage, in complete metamorphosis, the larva's body structure and systems are completely changed into its adult form.

rectum: part of the digestive system where wastes collect before passing out of the body

simple eyes: eyes only able to sense light from dark

sperm: male reproductive cell

spermatheca: (spur-muh-THEE-kuh) sac in female insects that stores sperm after mating

spiracles (SPIR-i-kehlz)**:** holes down the sides of the thorax and abdomen. They let air into and out of the body for breathing.

stinger: sharp-tipped needle to stab and deliver venom

thorax: the body part between an insect's head and abdomen

venom: poison produced by some insects to kill prey or attack enemies

DIGGING DEEPER

For more on hornets and other insect architects, explore these books and online sites.

BOOKS

Gifford, Clive. *Robotic Hornet: Learn How Hornets Have Inspired the Design of Robots—Then Build a Crawling Hornet with Light-Up Eyes and Flapping Wings!* Berkeley, CA: Silver Dolphin, 2005. Discover the science of biomimetics—creating machines and materials that copy nature. In this case, read about insects while following the directions to assemble a robotic hornet with a moving tail and fluttering wings.

Johnson, Sylvia. *Wasps.* Minneapolis: Lerner Publications Company, 1984. Full-color, close-up photos and text let you explore the lives of different kinds of wasps—hornets' close kin.

Miller, Sara Swan. *Ants, Bees, and Wasps of North America.* New York: Franklin Watts, 2003. Discover the traits that these insects—all belonging to the insect order Hymenoptera—share. Learn about different kinds of ants, bees, and wasps that live in North America.

Pohl, Kathleen, ed. *Potter Wasps.* Orlando, FL: Steck Vaughn, 1990. Investigate how a potter wasp builds its nest. Think how its construction techniques and its home are similar to a hornet's and how they're different.

WEBSITES

Hornets

http://www.academickids.com/encyclopedia/index.php/Hornet

    Find out more facts about hornets. And check out hornet myths, things people believe that are not true.

Hornets: Gentle Giants

http://www.vespa-crabro.de/horneets.htm

    Hear hornets and click to see photos.

Learning from Hornets

http://www.empa.ch/plugin/template/empa/*/30176/---/l=2

    This scientific site tells what scientists hope to learn by watching hornets build their nests.

HORNET ACTIVITIES

MAKE PAPER THE WAY A HORNET DOES

Hornets make paper by scraping up bits of wood, mixing them with their saliva, and spreading the mixture into a thin layer. You can make paper in a similar way. Only instead of grinding up wood, you'll start with newspaper. Newspaper is made from wood chips and recycled paper. So, just like hornets, you'll mix up wood pulp and make paper. This activity can be messy, so wear old clothes, work with an adult partner, and clean up when you're finished.

1. Tear 20 sheets of newspaper into tiny pieces, put in a bowl, and cover with water. Leave overnight.
2. Have your adult partner cut a 5-inch (13 cm) square of window screen (available at hardware stores). Cut 3 waxed paper squares of the same size. Spread out a plastic garbage bag in the kitchen. This will be your work area. Spread 3 paper towels on the garbage bag.
3. Pour 2 cups of the soaked newspaper and water into a blender. Add 1 tablespoon of cornstarch and blend until it looks like a gray milk shake.
4. Choose a bowl big enough to fit the screen square. Pour the paper pulp into the bowl. Place the screen flat on top of the pulp. Press it down until the screen disappears. Then lift the screen straight up.
5. Cover the pulp and screen with 1 sheet of the waxed paper. Flip it, waxed paper side down, onto 1 of the paper towels. Cover the screen with 3 more paper towels. Roll with a rolling pin. Remove the wet paper towels and screen. Repeat to make 2 more sheets of paper. Let dry overnight.

HOW DOES HORNET PAPER COMPARE TO MANUFACTURED TYPING PAPER?

Scientists wanted to examine the structure of the paper that hornets make. So they used a scanning electron microscope. That kind of microscope enlarges many, many times.

Take a look at the images below to see the structure of the hornet's paper for yourself. In what ways is the paper made by hornets like manufactured typing paper? How is it different?

INDEX

PHOTO ACKNOWLEDGMENTS

The images in this book are used with the permission of: © Tom McHugh/Photo Researchers, Inc., p. 4; © Dr. Elmar Billig, pp. 5, 17, 19, 21, 25, 26–27, 28, 31, 33; © Scott Camazine/Photo Researchers, Inc., p. 7 (top); © Ken Preston-Mafham/Premaphotos, p. 7 (bottom); © Warren Photographic, pp. 8–9, 15, 35; © Bill Hauser/Independent Picture Service, pp. 10–11; © Tim Shepherd/OSF/Animals Animals, p. 12; © NHPA/Stephen Dalton, p. 13; © Dr. John Brackenbury/Photo Researchers, Inc., p. 14; © Mark Preston-Mafham/Premaphotos, p. 23; © Oxford Scientific/Photolibrary, p. 29; © Yves Lanceau/Photo Researchers, Inc., p. 37; © Mauritius/Photolibrary, pp. 38–39; © Gerry Ellis/Minden Pictures, p. 41 (top); © Premaphotos/naturepl.com, p. 41 (middle); © Stephen Dalton/Minden Pictures, p. 41 (bottom); Skip Jeffery Photography, p. 47 (both).

Front Cover: © Patrick Bennett/CORBIS.